Silver Bullets
COLORADO
TM

Silver Bullets
COLORADO
TM
Coors LIGHT
JULIE CROTEAU
Silver Bullets
COLORADO
Coors
GINA SATRIANO
Silver Bullets
COLORADO
STACY SUNNY
Silver Bullets
COLORADO

The Colorado Silver Bullets

For the Love of the Game

Women Who Go Toe-To-Toe With The Men

by

Dave Kindred

Longstreet Press, Inc.
Atlanta, Georgia

Published by
LONGSTREET PRESS, INC.,
a subsidiary of Cox Newspapers,
a division of Cox Enterprises, Inc.
2140 Newmarket Parkway
Suite 118
Marietta, Georgia 30067

Printed in the United States of America

1st printing, 1995

Library of Congress Catalog Number 94-74228

ISBN: 1-56352-199-7

This book was printed by Horowitz/Rae, Fairfield, New Jersey

Color Separations and film preparation by Holland Graphics, Inc., Mableton, GA

Book design by Neil Hollingsworth
Cover photograph by Ben Crain
Special thanks to photographers Scott Cunningham, Tim O'Dell, Mark Gall, and Laura Wulf for the use of their work; to the Silver Bullets players who contributed personal photographs; and to Debra Larson, public relations director for the Bullets, for her help in pulling the pieces together.

. . . FOR THE LOVE OF THE GAME

Keri Kropke (L) and Ann Williams suit up for spring training.

Twenty women played professional baseball across America in the summer of 1994.

They were paid $20,000 for work that asked them to leave good jobs, leave their families and travel 25,000 miles through 27 states and Canada for 44 games against men's teams. "Basically, the job was 24 hours a day for six months," an infielder said, or $4.63 an hour in a summer when millionaire players and billionaire owners shut down major league baseball rather than let each other get even richer.

So maybe we should begin this unlikely story, "Once upon a time . . .."

Once upon a time, 20 women played baseball for the love of the game.

You were the Colorado Silver Bullets.

The Silver Bullets were instant hits with their fans.

It was July and you were on a bus in Iowa when someone said you were near the most famous corn field ever to give shelter to baseball's ghosts. So you made a detour down country dirt roads flanked by tall stands of corn made beautiful by golden tassels and green husks.

And there, perfect in the ways a baseball diamond is always perfect, its grass green and its dirt gold, you saw Shoeless Joe-Jackson's safe harbor. Children

Emerging from the stalks: (L-R) Julie Croteau, KC Clark, Melissa Coombes, Ann Williams, Jeanette Amado, Lynne Boring, Shannan Mitchem, Toni Heisler, Michelle Delloso.

played catch there. As the bus pulled to a stop, you felt a shiver of excitement. For a baseball player who understands the game's romance, this was hallowed ground.

Because Shoeless Joe and his White Sox teammates did it in the movie, you did it on this hot summer day. You walked out of the corn field and onto the outfield grass as if you were ghosts materializing for a game with friends from another time and another place. You walked onto the Field of Dreams. And in time you would say the summer of 1994 was a dream come true.

Shoeless Joe Jackson and his teammates from the movie "Field of Dreams."

The real "Field of Dreams" in Iowa.

Phil Niekro: "I had a box of Kleenex for them."

PHIL NIEKRO,
THE MANAGER:

"THE HARDEST THING WAS CUTTING PLAYERS. THEY ALL WANTED SO MUCH TO MAKE IT. I LEARNED THERE ARE 28 OR 29 DIFFERENT WAYS OF CRYING. I HAD BOXES OF KLEENEX FOR THEM. ONE WOMAN WOULDN'T LEAVE MY ROOM. SHE SAID SHE JUST COULDN'T HANDLE BEING CUT. THIS HAPPENED. SHE SAID SHE'D THROW HERSELF OUT THE WINDOW, AND WE WERE ON THE EIGHTH FLOOR. WE STAYED UP ALL NIGHT WITH HER BECAUSE SHE WAS SUICIDAL. WE FINALLY CALLED 911 TO TAKE CARE OF HER."

Those are pretty words: A dream comes true.

These are prettier words: Life becomes a dream.

Working in a world that had never existed for women, you played professional baseball.

You were on the road six months. You were 19th century barnstormers on a 21st century mission. Out of bed at 5 in the morning for the first plane to the next town. Suitcases never unpacked. No home games; no home ballpark. One long road trip, it was six months of baseball against men, against pros and amateurs, six months of baseball dreaming.

You came from every corner of the country: Arizona and Alabama, California, Michigan and Vermont. You came from college, bright and determined professionals with jobs as teachers and coaches, lawyers and firefighters. You were the women of a society's expectations—

Ann Williams, school teacher, became...

...Ann Williams, professional baseball pitcher.

until you heard the news.

Maybe someone telephoned you with the news. Or maybe you saw a note in the newspaper: *Someone's starting a women's professional baseball team*.

So you picked up and went. You put away the disguises ordered by society. You would be who you wanted to be: A ballplayer.

Open tryouts in Orlando, Florida, attracted a wide variety of aspirants.

Phil Niekro demonstrates how he holds his famous knuckleball.

If only you knew how to hold a baseball.

Really. How do you hold this thing?

You were 22 years old, a college graduate, an All-American softball player, an athlete from the day your father and mother attached a plastic basketball hoop to the crib. But you had never touched a baseball. For a girl, baseball didn't exist.

Ann Williams had been chosen from tryouts to become a pitcher. She walked up to Phil

Joe Niekro "communicating" with Ann Williams.

ANN WILLIAMS, PITCHER:

"ONE DAY JOE NIEKRO IS TELLING ME, 'FOLLOW THROUGH, FOLLOW THROUGH.' I KEPT FOLLOWING THROUGH, AND HE KEPT SAYING, 'FOLLOW THROUGH, ANN.' SO I GO, 'HMMM,' AND KEPT SNAPPING IT AND JOE SAYS, 'FOLLOW THROUGH.' I SAY, 'I AM SNAPPING IT!' AT WHICH POINT JOE STOPS ME AND SHOWS ME WHAT HE MEANS, LIKE HE'S TALKING TO A 6-YEAR-OLD LITTLE LEAGUER. HE MEANS TO BEND MY BACK AND REACH DOWN LOW AFTER DELIVERING THE PITCH. WHAT WE HAD WAS A LANGUAGE BARRIER. 'FOLLOW THROUGH' IN SOFTBALL MEANS SNAP YOUR WRIST. 'FOLLOW THROUGH' IN BASEBALL MEANS BEND YOUR BACK AND GET DOWN LOW. WE WERE FINE ONCE WE LEARNED EACH OTHER'S LANGUAGE."

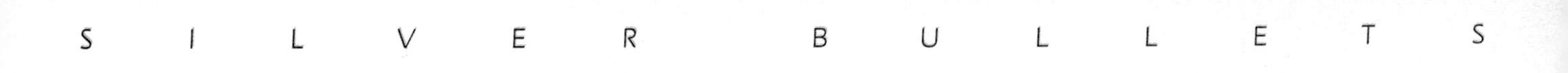

Niekro, the team manager, one of the best baseball pitchers in history, the winner of 318 games in 24 seasons, a man headed for the Hall of Fame. Williams went to Niekro with a baseball in her hand. "And I said, 'Phil, what's the best way to hold this?'"

Williams's concern came from her days as a softball second baseman and outfielder. There the ball was so big she held it back in her hand and put three fingers around it. That didn't work with the tiny baseball.

"Phil just looked at me and kinda smiled and said, 'Whatever's comfortable.' I finally got the ball out on the end of two fingers. The farther out you can get it, the quicker the release. But I didn't know that then."

When a coach, Tommy Jones, spoke about the virtues of soft hands on ground balls, meaning an infielder's hands should be moving toward the body as they accept the ball, Williams asked, "You mean we oughta cuddle it?" Jones was a baseball lifer. Eight years a player, 12 years a manager, a man who managed Bo Jackson and Cecil Fielder, he had never heard an infielder asked if he oughta cuddle a ground ball.

Coach Tommy Jones had never heard of "cuddling" a baseball.

"Yeah, I guess so — 'cuddle' the ball," Jones said. "That's what I want you to do. 'Cuddle' it."

You used curious words.

You asked curious questions.

You had never held a wooden bat.

You had never taken a lead off a base.

Not only had you never thrown a baseball, you had never seen one thrown toward you.

You had never made a double-play pivot in front of a 6-foot-

Five-foot tall Michele McAnany makes the double-play pivot at second.

Catchers try to adjust to the longer throw .

3 baserunner.

You had never run the 90 feet to first base, a distance, Red Smith once wrote, that is the nearest to perfection that man has yet achieved.

"Ninety feet," Ann Williams said, "felt like a quarter-mile."

Already smaller than men, you were further diminished by geometry. Moving first base from softball's 60 feet to baseball's 90 feet enlarges every dimension of the playing field. We should put into a male perspective the spatial reality that faced women moving from softball to baseball. Let's say that in the year 2027 the New York Yankees are barnstorming against the E.T. All-Stars. Because they play E.T.'s game on E.T.'s field, they immediately are intimidated and diminished. It's now 120 feet between bases; it's 200 feet from home to second, not 127 feet 3 3/8 inches; the outfield fences are 650 feet away.

E.T.'s pitcher is a creature 8 feet 5 inches tall who reaches 135 m.p.h. on the radar gun throwing a ball no bigger than a golf ball. It is a ball the Yankees have never touched in their baseball lives. They're trying to hit with bats made of a material foreign to their experience and 25 percent heavier, bats made from the heart wood of South African boab trees. Suddenly, it's a whole new ball game.

Small wonder the women

Coach Paul Blair addresses the troops at spring training.

"We'd never seen popups go so high."

found it unsettling.

"It was a circus act when we first went out there," said Jeanette Amado, a Silver Bullets outfielder. "Popups — we'd never seen popups go so high. We'd look like the Bad News Bears. It was brutal. The coaches would say, 'What are you women *doing*?'"

They weren't doing baseball.

Not the way men do it.

A guy's game, baseball. Maybe the first object a boy truly loves is his baseball glove. One boy loved his Rawlings glove, the Rip Repulski hinged-heel model. He took it to bed with him, took it to school, wore it attached to his belt just in case a game broke out at lunch time. Even a generation later, the boy had a picture by his typewriter. The boy in the picture is 10 years old and on his left hand is the Rip Repulski glove.

We grow up, boys do, knowing how to hold a baseball.

How do we know?

We just do.

Maybe we saw a picture in *SPORT* magazine of Bob Feller's fast ball grip. Maybe Dad held the ball out for us one day and we noticed how he did it and so we never had to ask the Ann Williams question. Maybe holding a baseball is part of the unspoken language that connects fathers and sons, a language denied to some fathers and daughters or some mothers and sons. More's the pity for that denial because parents and children need every connection

Allison Geatches: "The last thing I wanted to do was go home and play with dolls."

Shannan Mitchem:
"We want to be treated as baseball players."

SHANNAN MITCHEM:

"PEOPLE SEEMED TOO CAUGHT UP IN THE WOMEN-VS.-MEN THING AND REFUSED TO SEE IT AS ATHLETES AGAINST ATHLETES. WE WANT TO BE TREATED AS BASEBALL PLAYERS. SOMETIMES WE WERE TREATED AS SOMETHING LESS. THE MEN WERE ALWAYS POLITE IF THEY SLID INTO YOU. I WAS PLAYING THIRD BASE ONE NIGHT IN MADISON, WISCONSIN, AND A GUY SLID INTO ME, CLIPPED ME PRETTY GOOD. I WENT END OVER END. HE GOT UP AND PATTED ME ON THE REAR. THE WHOLE STANDS JUST WENT CRAZY BOOING AND YELLING AT HIM. ONE GUY GOES, 'HEY, THIS ISN'T HOCKEY.' I TOLD THE OTHER PLAYER IT WASN'T HIS FAULT. WHEN I PLAYED AGAINST WOMEN IN SOFTBALL, NO ONE APOLOGIZED FOR SLIDING INTO YOU. GIRLS ARE PLAIN MEAN."

they can make, especially a connection so enduring as that made by the sweet flight of a ball tossed back and forth.

Maybe you were a lucky girl and played catch with your father or a brother. "The last thing I wanted to do," said Allison Geatches, a Silver Bullets outfielder with five brothers, "was go home and play with dolls." Maybe you used Dad's old glove and you threw at his target, coming over the top, snapping your wrist.

"Dad never treated me like a daughter or a girl," outfielder Pam Schaffrath said. "He treated me like an athlete." You could throw a baseball.

"Dad and I would play catch in the snow in the front yard," said Elizabeth Burnham, a catcher whose father moved to Vermont from Brooklyn, leaving behind his beloved Dodgers. "The older I got," the catcher said, "the farther apart we got in the yard." Until, finally, Thomas Burnham admitted, "She threw too hard for me to handle anymore."

Pam Schaffrath: Dad "treated me like an athlete."

Elizabeth Burnham counseled by Joe Niekro.

KC Clark at age 9... and 15 years later as a professional.

A boy's game, baseball.

You learn that soon enough.

They let you play Little League maybe, even Babe Ruth.

From then on, only the boys can play. The girls watch.

Harvard University historian Doris Kearns Goodwin grew up keeping score at Dodgers games in the 1950s. She has confessed that baseball held her in thrall from then on.

"I am often teased (she once wrote) by my women friends about my obsession, but just as often, in the most unexpected places — in academic conferences, in literary discussions, at the most elegant dinner parties — I find other women just as crazily committed to baseball as I am, and the discovery creates an instant bond between us."

Like Doris Goodwin, Julie Croteau first went to a major league baseball game as a little girl. She was 8. The game was at Fenway Park. She carried her ball glove and she remembers walking down an aisle in the right field bleachers. She said to her parents, "I'm going to be a professional baseball player." No one told her that girls can only keep score.

Shortly she learned it on her own.

She was allowed to play in Little League and Babe Ruth League. "Then, when I was 11 or 12, the girls started disappearing," she said. Biology took over. Girls would become women and boys men. These certain developments cost girls their early superiority in athletics.

Even so, Julie Croteau didn't want to disappear: "I was very aware I was a girl. I knew the differences. I just didn't see how it mattered. I see myself as a baseball player, not a female baseball player."

She loved the game.

She couldn't remember ever not loving it.

Every year in high school, Croteau tried out for the boys' team. Every year she believed she was good enough to make the varsity. "I believed that eventually they would *see*." But every year she was cut. Her senior year, told again she wasn't good enough, she called home and

Julie Croteau: "I see myself as a baseball player, not a female baseball player."

In front of Phil Niekro's statue:
(L-R) Pitchers Lee Anne Ketcham, Deb Sroczynski,
Gina Satriano, Lisa Martinez, Ann Williams,
Bridget Venturi, and Shae Sloan.

SHAE SLOAN, PITCHER:

"ONE DAY I REALIZE WHAT'S HAPPENING. PHIL NIEKRO WAS THE MAN WHO GOT EVERYONE TO THE FIELD. HE BROUGHT PEOPLE TO THE STADIUM. HE IS ONE OF THE GREAT PITCHERS EVER. AND HE'S DRIVING OUR VAN! PHIL NIEKRO IS DRIVING OUR VAN AND I'M RIDING ALONG. WE'RE THE KEN GRIFFEYS AND NOLAN RYANS OF WOMEN'S BASEBALL, BUT WE'RE REALLY JUST PEONS IN THE GRAND SCHEME OF BASEBALL. THE QUESTION IS, 'WHAT CAN WE BECOME?' WE GOTTA STEP UP AND DO IT."

told her parents: "I don't want them to get away with it."

The family spent $10,000 on a sex-discrimination suit which they lost when a judge ruled that a girl had no constitutional right to play boys' baseball.

"People spit on me," Croteau said. "I was ostracized. It was horrible. By loving a sport, by wanting to play, I was made to feel I was bringing down the empire."

A boy's game. A man's game.

Men scratchin' and spittin' and cussin'.

It's Pete Rose's busted-up mug.

It's tobacco juice sliding down George Brett's chin.

The Hall of Fame catcher Roy Campanella once said, "To play this game good, a lot of you has got to be a little boy."

Phil Niekro with models as formation of the team was announced.

The real Pepper Davis, portrayed by actress Geena Davis in A League of Their Own.

"I was kind of watching my language at the start. Then one night one of our girls got called out. She went back to the dugout and somebody asked her what the pitch was. The girl who'd struck out said some curse words I'd been hearing all my life. I said, 'We've got ourselves a baseball team here.'"

—PHIL NIEKRO

It's a boy's game — but one day late in 1993 you heard that someone wanted to create a women's baseball team to play men's teams. Some games would be played in major league stadiums, some against minor leaguers.

You were skeptical. Baseball? Women? It had the odor of a publicity gimmick. Barnstorming in the 1930s, the Olympic track and field champion Babe Zaharias pitched to Babe Ruth. She struck him out. Big deal, Babe fans Babe. Just a stunt.

In the 1940s, with many big leaguers in World War II, promoters created the All-American Girls Professional Baseball League. It was more than a stunt, but just barely. The women didn't play men and didn't play baseball. The bases were less than 90 feet apart; the mound was closer than 60 feet 6 inches, and the ball was neither a baseball nor a softball but something in between. To make sure everyone knew what was being sold, the men who owned the league designed uniforms for the women. Not baseball uniforms. Skirts. Girlie shows on a circus midway showed little more thigh than these women did in a league of their own.

Baseball by women in 1994?

You were skeptical.

But what the hell.

Women had become astronauts and jet pilots. Why not baseball players?

Nancy Niekro, a baseball wife for almost 30 years, loved the idea. As her husband wondered if he ought to take the manager's job, she said, "Phil, go for it. It's a great idea. And it's about time."

So he did it.

And you did it.

You went to Florida for the tryouts.

You picked up a wooden bat for the first time. You met women who had left jobs and boyfriends and homes and families. They'd been All-Americans on college softball teams that won everything. But that was softball. This is a different game. This is the game America knows. No longer were you on the outside looking in at baseball. Now you were on the inside looking out at America. And no women had

The movie cast for A League of Their Own.

Michele McAnany: "...a gift from God."

MICHELE MCANANY, SECOND BASEMAN:

"TO BE ABLE TO PLAY BASEBALL IS A GIFT FROM GOD."

. . .

"WE WENT EVERYWHERE. TENNESSEE, SOUTH DAKOTA, BROADWAY. I LEARNED MORE HISTORY AND GEOGRAPHY AS A SILVER BULLET THAN I DID IN ALL MY HIGH SCHOOL AND COLLEGE DAYS. THE PENNSYLVANIA LACKAWANNA HOTEL USED TO BE A RAILROAD STATION. WE WENT TO HARVARD YARD. I GOT PICTURES OF ME AND THE GREEN MONSTER AT FENWAY PARK. IT WAS NEAT TO HEAR THE ACCENTS ALL OVER AMERICA."

ever been there before.

You were the first.

You would throw a curve ball.

At age 27, a college softball outfielder, Bridget Venturi became a pitcher with the Silver Bullets. Like Ann Williams, she had never thrown a baseball.

"The good thing was, I didn't have any bad habits to break," Venturi said with a smile. "I didn't have *any* habits."

She threw to a grizzled old guy named Joe Pignatano, once a major league catcher, who had volunteered to help Niekro with his collection of eager neophytes.

Then one day it happened.

"The curve ball came so slowly that it wasn't a sudden revelation," Venturi said. "But I do remember throwing the first one. It had really good rotation and it curved, it actually *curved*. I said, 'Piggie, it *curved*.'

"Now, Piggie's got this scratchy, Italian New York voice. So he says, 'Yuh, ya got good rotation on dat 'un.'

"And I say, 'Piggie, that sucker *moved*.' And I thought, 'Well, somebody noticed. I guess something's happening here.'"

Baseball's happening.

Phil Niekro watches Bridget Venturi's curveball.

No circus.

No skirts.

Just a couple hundred women happening to baseball.

And one Lisa Fritz.

Phil Niekro liked what he saw the first time he saw Lisa Fritz. He saw a big, strong slugger.

He saw someone who could hit a baseball a long way.

"She could *drive* it off the right field wall," Niekro said.

The skipper saw a hitter unlike any other hitter in camp. As it turned out, he was right. She was very much unlike any other

Lisa "Tootsie" Fritz (R) towered over the other players.

hitter in camp.

Lisa Fritz reported an age of 41, a weight of 250 (though the camp scales caught her at 274). She said her hometown was Cincinnati and she was out of work at the time. In a group of well-conditioned athletes rosy with the vibrancy of youth, Lisa Fritz stood out in significant ways. She reminded some of the Bullets of a movie in which Dustin Hoffman dressed as a woman to get a job. They called Lisa Fritz "Tootsie," as in "Tootsie's 12 shots deep into the bourbon already."

"She could really hit," Jeanette Amado said. "When she hit the ball, there was a different sound. You looked around, 'Who's *that* hitting?'"

No one saw Fritz anywhere but the ballpark. She slept in her car because, she said, she had no money. She never took a shower with players, never raised her voice above an airy whisper and always ate alone.

"Yeah, I wondered about her, always talking in that little whisper and all," Niekro said later. "I decided to find out. But I didn't want to insult her by just asking her if she was a man. So

I figured I'd get her mad and make her use her real voice." Here Niekro lowered his voice significantly. "I'd get her to say something like, 'MR. NIEKRO, DAMMIT, I AM TRYING TO GET IN SHAPE.' But she'd never raise her voice above that whispering thing."

When a Bullet put the Tootsie question to Niekro, the wise old denizen of a thousand baseball locker rooms first said, yes, he thought she was a girl.

So a second question was put to him: *Phil, have you ever seen a girl?*

With the passion of a manager in love with three-run home runs, Niekro said: *Aw, c'mon. She's just a big ol' girl.*

Alas, the skipper had to give the big ol' girl her release. She was just too big and too ol'. She couldn't run, she couldn't get in shape.

Two weeks later came word that Lisa Fritz had admitted it. Her name was Gerald Fritz. He said he needed the baseball job to pay for a sex-change operation.

"So I called the team together," Niekro said. "I said, 'I don't know how to tell you this, but

Phil Niekro: "Aw, c'mon. She's just a big ol' girl."

Life on the road was no bed of roses.

JOE NIEKRO, PITCHING COACH:

"WE'VE BEEN ON THE ROAD SIX MONTHS. WE'VE PLAYED IN A DIFFERENT PLACE EVERY NIGHT. WE'VE BEEN UP EARLY, CATCHING BUSES, CATCHING PLANES, CARRYING LUGGAGE, GETTING OUR BUTTS BEAT — AND THESE WOMEN NEVER COMPLAINED ONCE. ALL I KNOW FOR SURE IS THIS: 20 MEN COULD NEVER HAVE DONE WHAT THESE 20 WOMEN DID."

Lisa Fritz is not really a woman, she's a guy.' About seven of our girls jumped up and pointed at their teammates, saying things like, 'You owe me $10,' 'You owe me $20,' 'I *knew* it.'"

The night that "Inside Edition" made the Fritz story part of its tabloid-TV show, the Bullets watched in raucous amusement. As Niekro left the room, he looked back over his shoulder and said to his players, "I can't believe she had the balls to try that."

"Next year," said the coach, Tommy Jones, "we might ought to upgrade our medical exams."

Lisa was gone.

You stayed.

You were one of the 20 women who would suit up on the first women's professional baseball team of all time.

What to expect of a summer in which your life would become a dream?

No one knew.

No one had gone this way before. You would be the first and the trail would be yours to make and only you could ever say you went out there first. No one else. Just you. Only you could ever feel what it felt like.

"Spring training was getting toward the end," said Pam Schaffrath, "and the team was picked and I really realized what I was doing. It wasn't only the money. Not only playing baseball out there. Not only feeling like kids again, which was a great feeling. It was what we were doing as women — the first women to play professionally against men, and be noticed, and be respected.

"I was walking off the field and it hit me.

"I thought, 'Wow, we're doing this.'"

Pam Schaffrath giving hints to young fans.

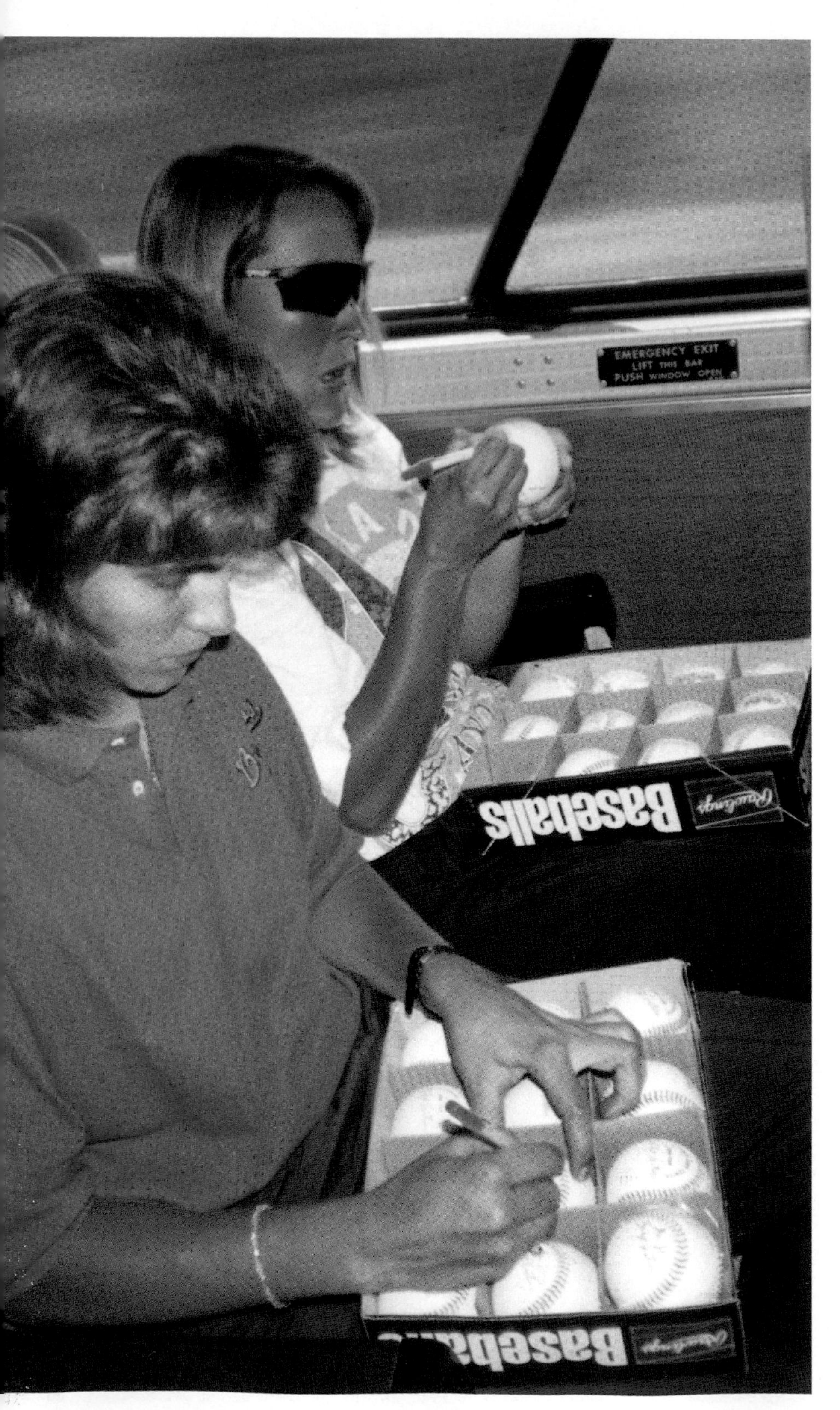

Another day, another bus trip: Shae Sloan (L), Melissa Coombes.

You were doing baseball.

Six months of moments you would remember: sweet moments, moments of fright and anxiety and disappointment, times when you needed your teammates to just shut up, moments of joy and despair you wanted to share and couldn't because only you had been there and only you had done it.

The infielder Shannan Mitchem, angry one day, took a ballpoint pen. She wrote a note on the back of her shoes.

Its armed-robber message: "Nobody Moves & Nobody Gets Hurt."

Laughter 1, Tears 0.

Six months of professional baseball, $4.63 an hour for six months, six months of plane rides and bus rides, late nights and early mornings, $1.99 dinners at Denny's, romance conducted by telephone from rooms in Watertown and Sioux Falls and Thunder Bay, the bus pulling up one morning to a godforsaken hotel somewhere in South Dakota.

You took one look and declared the place a seedy, musty

dump. Even by pioneer standards, this was too grungy.

Trudging off the bus, lugging bags, walking through dimly lit and narrow hallways, you and your baseball sisters arrived in a seedy musty dark grungy dump with no elevators. Your rooms were on the second floor up a twisting set of stairs. Each room came with a bed that by the headboard had a slot for quarters. "I thought they stopped making vibrating beds in the '70s," Shannan Mitchem said.

In Bowie, Maryland, there was no dressing room for the team to change.

The bus had gone to the wrong hotel. So everyone headed back downstairs. Rather than carry luggage down the narrow stairs, outfielder KC Clark raised a window and tossed her luggage onto the sidewalk below.

Six months on the road.

"A grueling grind," Lee Anne Ketcham said.

"Twenty-four hours a day for six months," Amado said.

"We've all aged seven dog years," Mitchem said.

You saw a million curve balls when you had never seen one in your life. Every day you worried. Could you really play this hard game, the game that always belonged to men? How good were you? Were you getting any better? What did Phil think?

You saw a million curve balls....

Six months.

Seeing the same faces. Hearing the same chatter, the same lame jokes, the same goof-offs goofing off. Whining, complaining, feeling sorry for themselves, telling everybody else in your Mom voice what they ought to be doing. Niekro was always talking about who'd you want in a foxhole with you. Would you want any of these women in a foxhole with you?

Some days the answer was no, no way, never.

Yet some days they were your sisters forever.

May 27, 1994, was such a day.

You were in St. Paul, Minn. Your team had lost its first six games by a cumulative score of 58-1. The bosses scaled back unrealistic plans of a season of games against minor league teams. The idea still was to play men's teams, but they would be over-30 rec leaguec teams and some college all-stars.

Talk about moments.

Your bus pulled up in the stadium parking lot where fans were tailgating in anticipation of the game. As you left the bus, everyone cheered. The public-address announcer welcomed the crowd to "gender-sensitive Municipal Stadium." When you came to bat, music played: "Let's Give 'Em Something to Talk About," and "There Is Nothing Like a Dame," and "Standing on the Corner, Watching All the Girls Go By."

With 3,954 people in the ballpark, you and your sisters beat the over-35 Richfield Rockets, 7-2, becoming the first women's professional baseball team to defeat men. The men's coach, Ron Cottone, a minister, said a thing that gave you chill bumps:

"The Silver Bullets showed that women are capable of playing the best game heaven ever invented. My hope is that young girls will see this and get it into their heads that they can do this."

You even did it with a flourish. Lee Anne Ketcham struck out the first two hitters in the last inning, her 12th and 13th strikeouts.

"Then I got two strikes on the last hitter," she said. "And everybody in the whole stadium was standing and screaming and yelling uncontrollably."

Lee Anne Ketcham: "And I blew a fastball by him."

Phil Niekro: "I don't think it'll be too long...."

PHIL NIEKRO, THE MANAGER:

"THERE ARE SOME WOMEN NOT TOO FAR AWAY FROM BEING ABLE TO PLAY IN THE MINOR LEAGUES. I'VE SEEN SOME ALREADY WHO ARE AS GOOD, OR ALMOST AS GOOD, AS SOME PLAYERS I'VE SEEN IN A MINOR LEAGUE SPRING TRAINING CAMP. I DON'T THINK IT'LL BE TOO LONG BEFORE A WOMAN IS IN A MINOR LEAGUE CAMP. SO AT THAT POINT SHE'S A PROSPECT. HOW LONG IT TAKES HER TO GET TO CLASS AA, CLASS AAA BALL, I DON'T KNOW. SAME WITH THE MEN PROSPECTS — YOU DON'T KNOW. WILL THERE BE A WOMAN IN THE BIG LEAGUES SOME DAY? I'M NOT GOING TO SAY THERE WON'T BE. I NEVER THOUGHT I'D SEE A WOMAN DRIVING IN THE INDY 500. THINGS CHANGE."

Screaming for one more strike.

"And I went to 3-and-2."

This was your World Series. It was your Bob Welch against Reggie Jackson. It was your moment for the ages coming in a Minnesota ballpark on a night in May in the summer of 1994.

"And I blew a fast ball by him," Ketcham said. "And the place went absolutely bonkers."

Reggie Jackson had two home runs the night of Oct. 18, 1977, when Ketcham's parents said it was bedtime.

Oh, no. Even at 7 she was old enough to know she wanted to see Reggie's last at-bat that night. She went to her bedroom and there turned on a little television set, a black-and-white set with poor reception. She kept the volume low so her parents wouldn't hear what she was up to.

Mr. October soon enough hit a third home run. There arose a muffled cheer from a little girl's bedroom. And in the summer of 1994 Lee Anne Ketcham said, "I knew right then I wanted to play this game I grew up loving."

Six months on the road.

It was Father's Day in Hickory, N.C.

You arranged a party for Phil

Tommy Jones, Joe and Phil Niekro at their Father's Day party.

Niekro and his coaches, Joe Niekro and Tommy Jones. From Bridget Venturi's journal of the summer, her account of that party:

"We were all dead-tired but it turned out to be well worth the effort. The best part was our gifts to them: heinous ties with matching hankies, Old Spice, cheesy mesh #1 Dad hats, Depends & a Babe/Trucker magazine. They all donned their hats and ties, and Joe in his Depends, for a very classic picture!

"Phil made a touching speech saying he couldn't pick 20 finer young ladies to be on his team and how much this means to him. Joe added that if he had another daughter, it would be any one of us. But TJ really let it out when he told us that his 2-year-old daughter, Sarah, told him 'Happy Father's Day' and it was very emotional and he said it is hard sometimes to keep the relationships straight because we are like daughters, sisters, friends and players to him. This isn't an ordinary baseball team and he's never had to deal with this before.

"Then Phil & Joe went around hugging everyone. . . . And then they acted like goofballs when

Life on the road: Toga night for (L-R) Bridget Venturi, Jeanette Amado, Shae Sloan, Melissa Coombes.

Shae, Gina Satriano and I serenaded them with 'You Are My Sunshine' in the parking lot. They started doing a little Hee-Haw/Polka dance just as silly as could be. Then they said to do a real polka they'd need the beat in double time and we obliged. Goofiness again. And then we did it in triple time. We were all hooting and hollering — it was great.

"Then to top it off, they did it in slow motion.

"Afterwards, Shae and I watched our pitching on tape and learned that we needed to drive lower and use those legs!

"Another great day in my dream life!"

"Emma," the Coors cardboard model for the Silver Bullets display, poses with (L-R) Shae Sloan, Kathleen Christie, Kevin Lewis, Bridget Venturi.

Gina Satriano: "It was breaking my heart."

GINA SATRIANO, PITCHER:

"MY FATHER HAD BEEN A MAJOR LEAGUE PLAYER AND I'D PITCHED IN MEN'S LEAGUES FOR YEARS. ONE DAY IN LOS ANGELES A TELEVISION SHOW ASKED ME TO COME ON AND TALK ABOUT BASEBALL. I WAS HAPPY TO DO IT. BUT THEN THEY WANTED TO SHOOT A GAME WITH ME PITCHING AGAINST THE CAST AND CREW. SO WE PLAYED ONE INNING OF SOLID BASE-BALL. AND THEN SOME GUY COMES TO BAT WEARING A SUIT OF ARMOR. AND THEY WANTED ME TO HIT HIM SO HE COULD CHARGE THE MOUND. WELL, I WOULDN'T DO IT. IT WAS BREAKING MY HEART. I LOVE THE GAME TOO MUCH TO TREAT IT THAT WAY."

The Silver Bullets didn't win again until July 8. A 16-game losing streak made their record 1-22. Outscored 162-24, they had been shut out 13 times, seven times in a row.

Choose a word: humiliated or embarrassed, depressed or ashamed. At one time or another, you felt it all. You were All-Americans at your game. But in this game, the men's game, its physics and dimensions conspired against you.

The ball moved too fast from them and too slowly from you. The men made the field look small. For you it was a prairie.

The manager Casey Stengel took a look at his 1962 New York Mets and said, "Can't anybody here play this game?"

The coach Tommy Jones, with more than 20 years in pro baseball, a man with a World Series on his resumé, took a look at the 1994 Silver Bullets and said, "What I did in the summer of 1994 was more important than anything I've ever done."

He came to camp a skeptic, intending only to help in tryouts as a favor to the team's general manager, Shereen Samonds, who had been the general manager at Jones's last team, the Class AA Orlando Cubs.

Joe Niekro works with pitcher Deb Sroczynski.

"Three or four weeks into it, I became intrigued," Jones said. "Not only with the surprising talent level and the energy level but with the purity of people wanting to play baseball for the love of the game.

"All of a sudden, I realized that

Shortstop Toni Heisler: Defense was the best part of their game.

everything that had disappeared from the game was present with these women. The purity of the game — how it was 50 years ago — that was what got me on board.

"I said to Phil: What a tremendous coaching challenge — and it was nice dealing with athletes who cared what you had to say," Jones said. "That's an unique quality today. Double-A and Triple-A players have *all* the answers. These women actually listened to you. They got these great big elephant ears."

Listening and doing, alas, are not the same thing.

"Our bat speed was so poor that anybody who threw 80 miles per hour overwhelmed us. We'd never seen sliders and curves before, so anybody who threw breaking stuff we couldn't handle it. So if it's a power pitcher, we're done. If it's junk, we're done. Our rally would be a walk, a bunt and an error by the shortstop. If we got two hits in an inning, it would be a rally of epic proportions.

"We're losing every night. We're losing because we're learning the game. And we're learning it in front of 8,000 people every night.

"But, and this was incredible, these women never lost their love and desire for the game. It was unbelievable. And they were always telling us coaches, 'Thank you.' In 20 years, I never had a player say thank you."

The boundaries of Tommy Jones's teaching reached even into the dugout where, one night in Bowie, Md., with the Silver Bullets losing, he heard the unusual baseball sound of ... singing.

They were singing in the dugout. The singing was a country song being sung by KC Clark, Toni Heisler and Shae Sloan, who stopped singing when they heard Tommy Jones say loudly and with no melody:

"*If you want to SING, take it OUTSIDE.*"

KC Clark began to cry.

Not from the scolding.

From laughing and trying not to be heard laughing.

"When Tommy went off, I yelped like a dog, 'Uh-oh, ohmigod, what are we doing? Now we're in big trouble,'" she said.

Turning away, Tommy Jones smiled. His worst-case desperadoes on this team were country singers. If that's as bad as it gets the rest of his career, he can live with that.

You do not sing in the dugout.

It's a baseball thing.

You learn these things quickly.

You began to learn them in the spring when Phil Niekro made a little speech. It came after an

Tommy Jones: No singing in the dugout.

Lisa Martinez receives hugs after throwing a no-hitter.

intrasquad game in which the Silver Bullets were excited by plays they made. From Venturi's journal, this entry dated March 12:

"Phil was a bit in shock of our on-field behavior. Basically, we looked like a softball team out there. He was trying to nicely tell us that without deflating our enthusiasm.

"He said, 'I don't think I've ever seen in baseball a team stand up on the dugout stairs the entire game. And I don't think I've ever seen the entire infield run over and high-5 someone after a great play. I was ready for the outfield to come in and do the same. We must act as if we expect to make those plays. Congratulations are done in the dugout.

"'I've never seen the whole team congratulate a runner crossing the plate. MAYBE you do it in the bottom of the ninth. And NEVER, in all the leagues I've played in, EVER have I seen a player jump into the arms of the third-base coach after hitting a triple. I think I even heard screaming!'

"We all laughed, even Phil, but it was true and we needed to hear it."

From the start, Niekro made it clear he would manage the Silver Bullets only if they were about baseball and not about sexploitation. He wanted nothing to do with a sideshow. The baseball would be done Niekro's way, seriously and professionally, or he would have no part of it.

Inevitably, because our society is sexist, there were questions about the organizers' intentions. The only women who ever played baseball for money had done it wearing skirts. In 1992 someone organized a women's pro basketball league in which the players would be required to work in Spandex bicycle shorts. Japanese photographers at spring training asked the Bullets to pose in swimsuits. A California newspaper printed a cartoon of women playing baseball in bikinis.

And the man who created the Silver Bullets, the man who had persisted in this dream for a decade, was a man who once did promotions for Ted Turner and the Atlanta Braves, a man who . . .

"I'm the man who put on 'Wet T-Shirt Night,'" Bob Hope said.

As early as 1984, Hope had tried to place a women's team in a Class A minor league. The stuffed shirts who run organized baseball told Hope to sit down and shut up. But women in baseball was an idea he didn't forget.

In 1993 the Coors Brewing Company wanted to create a mainstream marketing vehicle that would, in Hope's words, "change

Bob Hope: The man behind the dream.

Bridget Venturi and Joe Niekro horsing around.

As souvenirs for the coaching staff — Phil Niekro, Tommy Jones and Joe Niekro — the Silver Bullets posed for photographs after a practice session in the season's last week. Media and spectators were ordered to leave the Georgia Tech field for the private shoot. Later a Silver Bullet explained the mysterious goings-on:

"All of us posed smoking cigars because Phil's always smoking the things. Then we all did goofy third-base coaching signals in honor of Tommy. And we took off our shirts and posed in our sport bras for Joe."

the way people think." Coors came to Whittle Communications in Knoxville, Tenn., where Hope was president of Whittle's sports and event marketing division.

This time Hope sold his idea. Coors put up $2.6 million for the first year.

The Silver Bullets would play baseball.

But not in tank tops and bicycle shorts.

Hope had become the gender-sensitive father of two daughters, Clair and Betsy.

"Men in this country have this odd double-track in their attitude toward women," Hope said. "You respect them as people and yet you grow up reading *Playboy* and you definitely see them almost as toys. Then, suddenly, when you have daughters, the harsh realization sets in: These are humans.

"You also see their struggles to get opportunities that come naturally to boys. If you're a boy, it's a clear track. If you're good enough, you play football; if you're not good enough for football, you play basketball or baseball; if you're really good, you play all three.

"It's just not that clear for

A night out: (L-R) Michelle Delloso, Shannan Mitchem, Bob Hope, Bridget Venturi, Katrina Warner of Reebok.

little girls. They're always torn between, Is it OK to run track? Is tennis OK? Is golf really OK? If I go out for soccer, where does that fit in with being a cheerleader? You go through their struggles — and they're more emotional, anyway, so it just brings you into their world and you struggle with them.

"It brings a whole new appreciation into your life of what they have to go through. Like we were at a party and somebody sort of nudged me and said, 'Look at that blonde over there.' It was Betsy, my oldest daughter."

You do not wear bikinis in

baseball.

You do not sing in the dugout.

You do not high-five on the infield and you NEVER, for ANY REASON, throw yourself into the third-base coach's arms.

These are baseball things the Silver Bullets learned.

They also learned to play.

Bridget Venturi noticed how her fast ball became a sinker when she gripped the ball with the seams rather than across them. "All of a sudden — wow, this was a sudden revelation — I had a sinker. And almost a screwball at the same time. It would sometimes sink and sometimes screw and sometimes do both. Wow."

Stacy Sunny, third baseman: "In softball, you just step and poke the ball in different places. But in baseball, you can't get away with that. You really have to put your hips into it to drive the ball. In throwing as well, you really use your legs and shoulders. So many little things to learn in baseball, like reading the ball off the bat. You have so much more ground to cover, you need quicker feet than in softball."

Michele McAnany, second baseman: "The most improved thing we did was infield practice. Really. In spring training, when we first started infield practice, it was a nightmare. We couldn't throw the ball anywhere. But by the end of the season, even our opponents said that if they gave runs for how well you took infield, we'd start every game one run ahead."

Elizabeth Burnham, catcher: "My best game was in Thunder Bay, Ontario. Beanie (Lee Anne Ketcham) was pitching. We won 5-0 and I felt really good with my game. I threw a runner out at second and picked one off first. Beanie threw a lot of dirt balls and I dug 'em all out. The best thing

Julie Croteau trying for two.

was a ground ball to the infield and I was backing up first when it turned out to be a bad throw — so I went down, sliding on one shinguard, and caught it to keep the guy from advancing. That was fun. I almost broke out laughing."

Kim Braatz, outfielder: "The thrill of running, diving, make a catch — what a feeling. There's nothing like it. One night I had three assists and this little boy came up to me after the game. He said, 'I saw Michael Jordan play right field, and you're much better than he is.'"

Stacy Sunny: "You need quicker feet...."

Michele McAnany: Steady improvement came in all areas of the game.

Elizabeth Burnham with Giants' Matt Williams...

...and with the Royals' Dave Henderson.

On July 8, 1994, the Silver Bullets won their second game, 6-0, and did it with Lisa Martinez pitching a no-hitter to beat the Summerville Yankees, the champions of an over-30 amateur league in Charleston, S.C. And not just an ordinary no-hitter at that — Martinez used her underhand softball delivery to rack up eight strikeouts.

Phil Niekro has seen everything. (During a playing of the national anthem, he told a Bullet, "I've heard this song so many times I can hum it in five languages.") He called Martinez's no-hitter "the most exciting damn thing I've ever seen in baseball."

Martinez, at age 30, had pitched dozens of softball no-hitters and perfect games. "About the fifth inning that night, I glanced down at the scorebook and, oh, wow, nobody had got a hit yet. It was like hush-hush about it on the bench. At the end of the game, I was so excited I ran to Elizabeth Burnham and just hugged her and said, 'Yeah.' Then the whole team was out there and we just all celebrated."

Throughout the summer, the men across the diamond came to say nice things about the Silver Bullets: "They're pretty smooth. I'm surprised." "They're good and they're only going to get better." "Surprising pitching and defense." "Fundamentally sound." "If she was a guy, her fast ball would be in the mid-90s. As is, she is tough." "Got some talent."

On their best nights, the Silver Bullets may have been the match for a men's junior college team. Someday, maybe a day in the near future, a woman will pitch in the minor leagues: Lee Anne Ketcham might do it; Niekro said a Class AA manager offered to trade his closer straight-up for Lisa Martinez.

In 1986 the Bullets' pitcher Gina Satriano worked out in major league tryouts, her fast ball hitting 78 m.p.h.; the daughter of a big league player and a district attorney when the Bullets called, Satriano believes a woman will pitch in the major leagues "in our lifetimes, maybe in the next 10 years."

Bob Hope: "I remember what Henry Aaron once said. 'Somewhere there's a woman who can play second base in the major leagues.'"

The Silver Bullets' numbers improved as the season wore on. In the 1-22 start, the average score was 7-1; they were shut out 13 times. They finished winning five of the last 21 games, the average score 6-2; they were shut out three times.

Lisa Martinez: An underhanded no-hitter.

Gina Satriano: From District Attorney...

...to pitcher for the Silver Bullets.

Certainly it hurt to lose so often by such scores.

But did it matter?

"In Memphis before a game, one of the Memphis Chicks came up to me," said outfielder Keri Kropke. "This Double-A player said, 'I can't believe you guys are making more money than we are. That's b.s.' I looked at him and said, 'Now you know how it feels when women make 65 cents for every dollar a man makes.' He went, 'Uh-oh, you got me.' From there on, we rapped and had a good time."

At Candlestick Park the Giants' great player, Barry Bonds, asked for autographs, posed for pictures, spotted Shannan Mitchem with a touch of mascara on her eyes and said, "Look, she's wearing makeup."

To which a Bullet replied, "Whattya think, Barry, it weighs her down? Look at you with that earring."

In the summer of 1994 you walked in from Shoeless Joe's cornfield in Iowa. You stood in front of the left field wall at Fenway Park.

You posed by Henry Aaron's

locker.

At the Oakland Coliseum, you stood in a corridor under the stadium and heard hundreds of fans chanting, "We want the Bullets . . . We want the Bullets." There were 23,567 people in the ballpark that day. You drew 30,978 in San Diego.

You came to believe what Michele McAnany said: "People love us. They love the underdogs, and nobody was ever more the underdog than us."

There were 33,179 people at Mile High Stadium in Denver, all standing to applaud you. "It was bigger than life, like a movie," McAnany said. "The place was filled and they shot off fireworks. It was electrifying. It just gave me the willies. It's so much fun, so many people thinking that what you're doing is one of the neatest things in the world."

What you did was baseball.

And more.

Ketcham: "It's opening doors."

Kim Braatz: "It's opening eyes."

Schaffrath: "A little girl thanked me for giving her somebody to look up to. That's what it's all about." The team's publicist, Kathleen Christie: "Boys, too, see this happening and they grow up with a different concept of women." Tommy Jones: "I see it now through the eyes of young daughters. It's a mission."

Bob Hope said, "I'd rather own the Silver Bullets than the New York Yankees. For two reasons — first, the Silver Bullets are unique. They're a more important team. This is a team of half the human race. Symbolically it means an awful lot. It says, 'Hey, it's OK for people who want to do something, who have been held back in the past, to give it a shot.'

"Second, the Silver Bullets make you feel like you're doing

Superstar Barry Bonds chats with Melissa Coombes, and Ann Williams.

Giants manager Dusty Baker surrounded by Silver Bullets in Candlestick Park.

THE SILVER BULLETS' BEST CROWDS IN 1994

42,082	AT CANDLESTICK PARK, SAN FRANCISCO
33,179	AT MILE HIGH STADIUM, DENVER
30,978	AT JACK MURPHY STADIUM, SAN DIEGO
23,567	AT MEMORIAL COLISEUM, OAKLAND

something worthwhile with your life. There's no immortality unless occasionally you can do something that really has some meaning. This team has meaning. It's also a team that wants to play baseball. There is a joy in their hearts."

A crowd of more than 33,000 turned out at Denver's Mile High Stadium.

You never dreamed this.

Boys kept playing baseball. Girls disappeared.

You never hoped this would happen because there was nothing in the culture's history as foundation for such a hope. Women didn't become professional baseball players. End of story.

Third baseman Shannan Mitchem signs autographs for enthusiastic fans.

Maybe you walked with your parents into a ballpark. Julie Croteau walked into Fenway Park's right field bleachers. She was 8 and she said with a child's naivete', "I'm going to be a professional baseball player." Shannan Mitchem's first-grade yearbook, long forgotten, was discovered in a closet and on an autograph page her sister, Kandy, had written, "I know someday you'll be a professional baseball player."

Julie Croteau takes a lead off first base.

And in the summer of 1994, Croteau walked with the Silver Bullets into Fenway Park for a game. She looked out to right field and there the adult saw the spot where the child once walked. Mitchem read and re-read that first-grade inscription. She said, "It was eerie. I didn't remember it at all. But obviously what I felt about baseball — it was my first love and always will be my greatest love — other people saw."

This was life becoming a dream. And it was even better than that, for dreams go away and life stays. This summer became part of you and it will

Lee Anne Ketcham: Contract ahead?

When the Silver Bullets play a 1995 game in Cincinnati's Riverfront Stadium, they'll be there thanks to the intervention of Reds' owner Marge Schott.

"The stadium wasn't going to have us," said Tommy Jones, the team's new general manager, "but then Marge heard about it and said she wanted the Silver Bullets to play there and wanted Lee Anne Ketcham to pitch. And she said, 'If this Lee Anne Ketcham is as good as you say she is, I'll sign her to a minor league contract at the end of your season.'"

always be there to remind you of who you are, reminding you that, yes, the summer of baseball in 1994 was hard but it was supposed to be hard because it's the hard that makes it great.

Before the last game of the season, Phil Niekro spoke to the Silver Bullets in the clubhouse. He told you how proud he was. He said no 20 men could have made it through such a season. He called you true warriors and said he'd have you in his foxhole anytime. With that he cried a little. Everyone cried a little, everyone together.

Something had happened in that summer, something largely beyond explanation, something that changed people, that touched them in ways they didn't know they could be touched. Bridget Venturi said:

"We were all, for some reason or another, brought together from these 30 different walks of life, to accomplish this one goal, to challenge history, to do something no one ever thought could be done.

"The common bond, the special memory we'll have of each

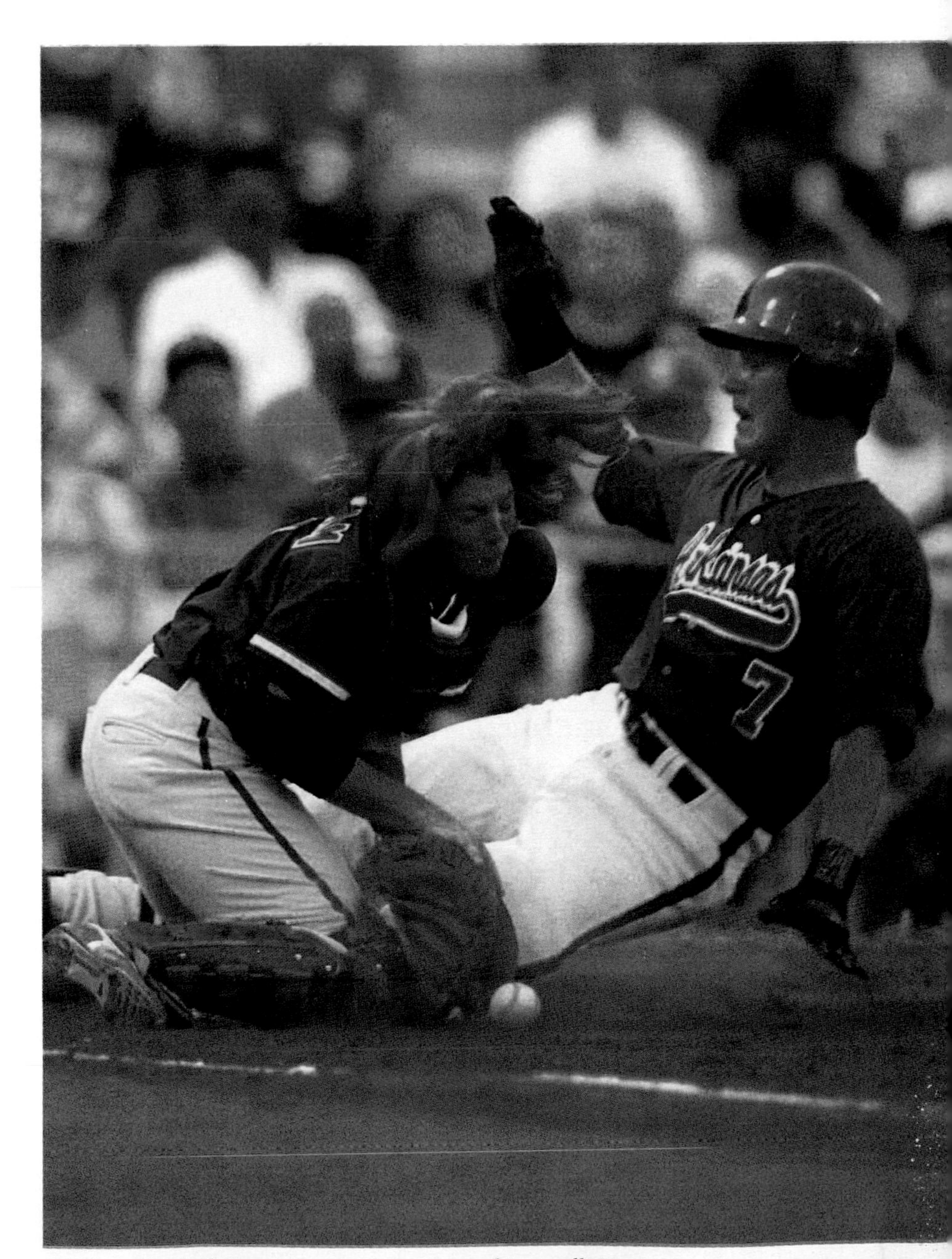

Catcher Elizabeth Burnham stands her ground in a collision at the plate.

person involved in this team — it's so difficult to explain, how special this is. The greatest souvenir we can have is that only we understand what it really is. I don't think any picture book or any novel or movie could ever capture that.

"You come together in spring training and you're going to start on this journey that no one has ever made before. And you're going to play men across the country. And everyone thinks you're crazy. And on Day 1 you don't have a chance or on Day 35 or Day 69. But maybe on Day 180 you might have a chance.

"For me the moments of pure joy were every moment on that field, just being out there. Whatever else was happening, on the field I knew I'd be happy. It was the best summer of my life because we did it and we were the first. And we'll do it again next year because this isn't the end. This is only the end of the beginning."

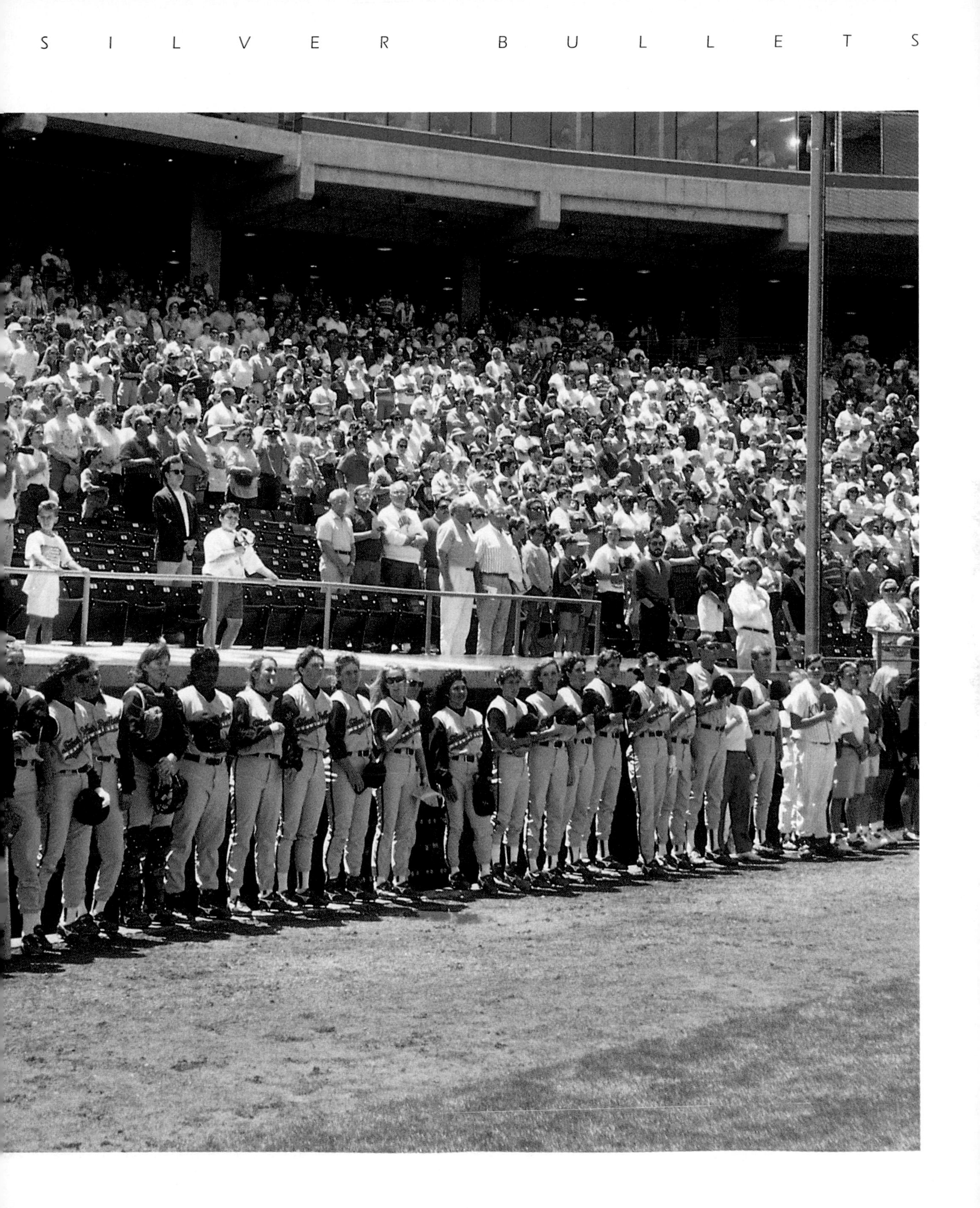

THE PLAYERS

Front Row: (L-R) Lee Anne Ketcham, Pam Schaffrath, Jeanette Amado, Julie Croteau, Lisa Martinez, Ann Williams, KC Clark, Michelle Delloso, Stacy Sunny, Michele McAnany, Elizabeth Burnham. Back Row: Joe Niekro, Tommy Jones, John Niekro, Toni Heisler, Shannan Mitchem, Allison Geatches, Shae Sloan, Keri Kropke, Gina Satriano, Bridget Venturi, Melissa Coombes, Phil Niekro.

Jeanette Amado

Position: ....Outfielder

Born: 12/12/65

Birthplace: ....Los Angeles, CA

Ht: ....5'2"

Wt: 130

Bats: ....Right

Throws: ....Right

Resides: ....Phoenix, AZ

College: .....University of Arizonz, 1988

A patient hitter who drew 11 walks in 48 trips to the plate this year, Jeanette was second on the Silver Bullets with an on-base percentage of .388. Her best game at the plate came early in the season at Mesa, AZ, where she went 2-3. She also played well in the field, committing only two errors in 26 games. An outstanding college softball player who hit .310 in four years at the University of Arizona, Jeanette led the Wildcats to a third place finish in the 1998 NCAA World Series. She coached a high school team to the Arizona State title in 1990.

SB

Kim Braatz

Position: .... Outfielder

Born: 7/13/69

Birthplace: .... Santa Ana, CA

Ht: .... 5'7"

Wt: 140

Bats: .... Right

Throws: .... Right

Resides: .... Albuquerque, NM

College: University of New Mexico, 1991

Kim missed half of the Silver Bullets inaugural season after sustaining a back injury that required surgery. Prior to her injury, she distinguished herself as an outstanding defensive right fielder. Although she missed half the season, she still tied for the team lead in assists by an outfielder. Kim earned second team All-American honors as a softball player at the University of New Mexico in 1990. She spent 1993 hitting .466 for a professional softball team and coaching an 18-and-under team in Novaro, Italy.

Elizabeth Burnham

Position: ....Catcher
Born: 12/28/70
Birthplace: ....Norfolk, CT
Ht: ....5'7"
Wt: 160
Bats: ....Right
Throws: ....Right
Resides: ....Newbury, VT
College: ....Lyndon State

Elizabeth turned out to be one of the pleasant surprises of the Silver Bullets inaugural season. She emerged as the team's regular catcher early in the year, and she developed into a dependable player at a challenging position. Elizabeth caught five base runners attempting to steal and was charged with only two passed balls in 35 games behind the plate. She also drove home six runs during the season. A starter as a freshman at the University of Connecticut in 1989, she moved on to become a two-time team MVP at Lyndon State.

00

KC Clark

Position: ....Outfielder

Born: 10/10/69

Birthplace: ....Sacramento, CA

Ht: ....5'4"

Wt: 112

Bats: ....Right

Throws: ....Right

Resides: ....Rancho Cordova, CA

College: ....Cal. State Fullerton

KC was one of the fastest and quickest players on the inaugural Silver Bullets team, and she used those attributes to become a frequent starter in center field. Her speed and quickness enabled her to cover a lot of ground defensively in the outfield. She finished the 1994 season ranked second on the team in both put-outs and chances among the team's outfielders. KC played Little League baseball for seven years until she was 14 years old. She patrolled center field for Fullerton State's softball team in both 1991 and 1992.

SB
Silver Bullets

Melissa Coombes

Position: ....Pitcher, First Base

Born: 6/7/68

Birthplace: ....San Gabriel, CA

Ht: ....5'6"

Wt: 145

Bats: ....Left

Throws: ....Left

Resides: ....Arcadia, CA

College: ....Cal. State Fullerton

Melissa was the only left-hander on the Silver Bullets pitching staff in 1994, and she finished second on the team in both games started and completed. She walked only 10 batters and struck out 21 in 47 innings of work, and she was very effective at holding runners close on the base paths. She did not commit an error in 14 games as a pitcher. Melissa also was an offensive force. Her .222 batting average was best on the team, and she had an on-base percentage of .333. She was a first-team All-American at Fullerton State in 1989.

Julie Croteau

Position: ....First Base

Born: 12/4/70

Birthplace: ....Berkeley, CA

Ht: ....5'8"

Wt: 130

Bats: ....Left

Throws: ....Left

Resides: ....Manassas, VA

College: ....St. Mary's, MD, 1993

Julie dazzled fans and opponents with her defensive prowess around the bag at first base last year. She posted a .990 fielding percentage and committed only two errors in 29 games while leading the Silver Bullets in put-outs. She also was involved in a team-high 21 double plays. As one of only two hitters on the team with more walks than strikeouts, she displayed a good eye and patience at the plate. Julie became the first woman to play NCAA baseball in 1989 at St. Mary's College in Maryland. She played three years of college baseball.

Michelle Delloso

Position: ....Second Base, Utility

Born: 1/12/69

Birthplace: ....Lansdale, PA

Ht: ....5'5"

Wt: 133

Bats: ....Right

Throws: ....Right

Resides: ....Lexington, SC

College: ....South Carolina, 1991

Michelle was one of the most versatile of all the Silver Bullets in 1994. She saw action at second base, shortstop, third base and in right field, more positions than any player on the team. She did not make an error in nine games as an outfielder. An excellent all-around athlete who earned multiple honors at both the high school and collegiate level, Michelle was a three-time NCAA All-American second baseman at the University of South Carolina. She compiled a .320 batting average and drove home 121 runs in four years there.

Allison Geatches

Position: ....First Base, Outfield

Born: 11/19/63

Birthplace: ....Mt. Clemens, MI

Ht: ....6'1"

Wt: 162

Bats: ....Right

Throws: ....Right

Resides: ....Mt. Clemens, MI

College: ....Detroit

Allison started several games at both first base and right field for the Silver Bullets in 1994. She played 18 games at first and 14 in the outfield. She handled all but three of 96 chances as a first baseman, and her strong right arm kept base runners honest when she played the outfield. An outstanding all-around athlete, Allison was a Parade and Street & Smith All-American basketball player as well as an all-state softball and volleyball competitor in high school. She also has international experience at the semipro level in basketball.

Toni Heisler

Position: ....Shortstop

Born: 5/6/69

Birthplace: ....Sacramento, CA

Ht: ....5'9"

Wt: 143

Bats: ....Right

Throws: ....Right

Resides: ....Elk Grove, CA

College: ....Cal. State-Sacramento

Toni started almost every game at shortstop for the Silver Bullets once she earned the job shortly after the start of the season. The team leader in assists, she took part in 19 double plays during the season, including three in an August contest at Tacoma, WA. Toni helped lead Sacramento State to the NCAA Division II finals in 1989. She took the Italian Softball Federation by storm in 1992 when she posted a .448 batting average while leading that league in batting, home runs, RBIs, stolen bases, runs scored and total bases.

Lee Anne Ketcham

Position: ....Pitcher

Born: 11/18/69

Birthplace: ....Tallahassee, FL

Ht: ....5'4"

Wt: 150

Bats: ....Right

Throws: ....Right

Resides: ....Birmingham, AL

College: ....Oklahoma State., 1993

Beanie" was the ace of the Silver Bullets pitching staff in 1994. The leader in earned run average, she had five wins and seven complete games including a shutout against an all-star team at Thunder Bay, Ontario. She struck out 14 batters in seven innings to lead the team to its first victory ever at St. Paul, MN, in May. Lee Anne struck out 62 batters and walked only 19 in 75 innings of work. A three-time academic All-Big Eight choice at Oklahoma State, she played shortstop on four straight conference championship softball teams there.

KETCHAM
44

Keri Kropke

Position: ....Outfielder

Born: 9/23/71

Birthplace: ....Montebello, CA

Ht: ....5'11"

Wt: 147

Bats: ....Right

Throws: ....Right

Resides: ....Whittier, CA

College: ......California (Berkeley), 1993

Keri was the only member of the Silver Bullets to play the entire 1994 season without committing an error. She also threw out two base runners from her outfield position during the season. She earned standing ovations from a huge crowd at San Diego's Jack Murphy Stadium for a pair of spectacular catches she made there. Keri was second on the team in doubles, and she was 2-2 in stolen base attempts. An All-American softball player at Cal-Berkley in 1993, she set school records there for triples, stolen bases and walks.

TBS
46

Lisa Martinez

Position: ....Pitcher

Born: 7/23/64

Birthplace: ....Stockton, CA

Ht: ....5'6"

Wt: 130

Bats: ....Both

Throws: ....Right

Resides: ....Stockton, CA

College: ....California (Berkeley), 1986

Lisa baffled many batters during the 1994 season with her variety of underhand offerings, but none more than the Summerville Yankees. She pitched a no-hitter against that Charleston, SC, team as the Silver Bullets recorded a 6-0 victory there in July. The only underhand pitcher on the team, Lisa was second on the staff in strike-outs and third in earned run average. A veteran of both international and intercollegiate softball wars, she played college ball at Cal-Berkeley and Texas A&M. She was Texas State Athlete of the Year in 1981.

Michele McAnany

Position: ....Second Base

Born: 11/15/63

Birthplace: ....Inglewood, CA

Ht: ....5'0"

Wt: 110

Bats: ....Right

Throws: ....Right

Resides: ....Culver City, CA

College: ..Cal State - Northridge, 1987

Michele led the Silver Bullets in on-base percentage and finished second in hits, RBIs and batting average while hitting in the lead-off spot most of the 1994 season. She doubled home the winning run in the final inning of the Silver Bullets 3-2 win at Watertown, NY, in August. Michele also helped turn 18 double plays while playing a solid second base throughout the summer. A two-time All-American who led Cal State-Northridge to the NCAA Division II softball titles in 1983, '84 and '85, she is a member of that school's Hall of Fame.

Shannan Mitchem

Position: ....Third Base

Born: 3/17/70

Birthplace: ....Decatur, GA

Ht: ....5'8"

Wt: 140

Bats: ....Right

Throws: ....Right

Resides: ....Stone Mountain, GA

College: ....Florida State, 1992

Shannan saw action at third base, right field and as the Silver Bullets' designated hitter during the 1994 season. She finished the year ranked fourth on the team in both batting average and on-base percentage. Shannan drove home the Silver Bullets' first run of the season with an RBI single at Tucson, AZ, and she finished on a high note by going 2-3 in the season finale in front of numerous hometown fans in Atlanta, GA. The starting third baseman for four years at Florida State, she played in the 1990, '91 and '92 NCAA World Series.

Gina Satriano

Position: ....Pitcher

Born: 12/17/65

Birthplace: ....North Hollywood, CA

Ht: ....5'7"

Wt: 165

Bats: ....Right

Throws: ....Right

Resides: ....Malibu, CA

College: ....California (Davis), 1988

Gina made 14 pitching appearances, including three as a starter, for the Silver Bullets in 1994. She posted the second best earned run average on the staff by keeping batters off balance with a variety of breaking pitches. Gina has been playing baseball most of her life with some softball thrown in. A deputy district attorney in Compton, CA, who earned her law degree from Pepperdine, she put her legal career on hold temporarily to join the Silver Bullets. Her father, Tom, played professionally for the Angels and Red Sox from 1961-70.

SATRIANO
42

Pam Schaffrath

Position: Outfielder, Designated hitter

Born: 4/25/71

Birthplace: ....Chicago, IL

Ht: ....5'8"

Wt: 150

Bats: ....Right

Throws: ....Right

Resides: ....Chicago, IL

College: ....Drake University, 1993

Pam tied for the Silver Bullets team lead in both doubles and stolen bases during the 1994 season. An outfielder who also saw action as the team's designated hitter, she finished third in base hits, official at bats and games played. Pam committed only three errors, and she was one of four Silver Bullet outfielders to throw out an opposing base runner. Named Drake University's top athlete for leading the Bulldogs to the Missouri Valley conference title in 1993, she hit 16 home runs and drove home 115 runs in her four seasons there.

Shae Sloan

Position: ....Shortstop, Pitcher

Born: 8/1/71

Birthplace:...................Huntsville, TX

Ht: ....5'10"

Wt: 150

Bats: ....Right

Throws: ....Right

Resides: ....Splendora, TX

College: ....Nebraska

Shae had one complete game in nine starts as a member of the Silver Bullets pitching staff in 1994. She did not allow a home run or hit a batter in the 37 innings she worked on the mound, and she also played errorless ball as a pitcher. She displayed great patience as a hitter, drawing seven walks in 15 trips to the plate. A four-year starter at shortstop for Nebraska, Shae earned All-Big Eight honors as the team captain in 1993. She made first team all-district as a junior and senior while playing for a high school boys team in Texas.

Deb Sroczynski

Position: ....Pitcher

Born: 8/20/67

Birthplace: ....Providence, RI

Ht: ....5'3"

Wt: 126

Bats: ....Right

Throws: ....Right

Resides: ....Taunton, MA

College: ....Bridgewater State

Deb was cut from the Silver Bullets squad in spring training, but she got another chance after attending a summer tryout session at Watertown, NY. She was the only one of more than 500 candidates who attended various summer camps to be asked to join the team this year. Deb pitched in two games without earning a decision after joining the team. A shortstop on Bridgewater State's conference champions, she has earned all-conference and all-academic honors there. She is also a regional black-belt karate champion.

SB
BIKE

Stacy Sunny

Position: ....Catcher, Third Base

Born: 12/13/65

Birthplace: ....San Bernadino, CA

Ht: ....5'6"

Wt: 135

Bats: ....Right

Throws: ....Right

Resides: ....Huntington Beach, CA

College: ....UCLA, 1989

Stacy led the Silver Bullets in games played, at bats, runs, hits, doubles, triples and RBIs during the 1994 season. The Silver Bullets' starting catcher at the beginning of the year who played most of the season at third base, she had three hits against the minor league Ogden Raptors in August. Stacy was named to the NCAA Division I All-Decade team for the 1980s following her career at UCLA and Nebraska. She was working as a freelance TV and film producer/assistant director prior to joining the Silver Bullets.

Bridget Venturi

Position: ....Pitcher, Outfielder

Born: 8/8/66

Birthplace: ....Highland Park, IL

Ht: ....5'10"

Wt: 155

Bats: ....Right

Throws: ....Right

Resides: ....Highland Park, IL

College: ....Michigan, 1989

Bridget played as both an outfielder and a pitcher for the Silver Bullets during their inaugural season. She made 10 appearances on the mound, one as a starter. An exceptional all-around athlete, she won the American Gladiators Grand Championship in 1990. Bridget earned an undergraduate degree in industrial engineering from Michigan and an MBA in International Business from DePaul. Once an international softball coach, she was an athletic scouting director for College Prospects of America before joining the Silver Bullets.

SB
BIKE
Mizuno
BIKE

Ann Williams

Position: ....Pitcher

Born: 9/18/70

Birthplace: ....Vero Beach, FL

Ht: ....5'7"

Wt: 138

Bats: ....Left

Throws: ....Right

Resides: ....Altamonte Springs, FL

College: ....Nicholls State, 1992

Ann made 12 pitching appearances, 10 in relief, for the Silver Bullets in 1994. She struck out 23 batters in 21 innings of work, the best ratio on the team. Her first start came at Watertown, NY, where she struck out seven batters in just 4 1/3 innings of work. She was the only Silver Bullets pitcher to hold opposing hitters under a .300 batting average. An excellent pinch-hitter with a good knowledge of the strike zone, Ann had a .333 on-base percentage. She earned All-Southland Conference honors as a senior at Nicholls State.

Bullets
COLORADO

Coaching Staff

(L-R) Joe Niekro, Phil Niekro, John Niekro, Tommy Jones, Jerry Thurston, Paul Blair, Joe Pignatano

Phil Niekro

Phil was the 14th winningest pitcher in the history of major league baseball during a legendary career that spanned 24 seasons. The winner of 318 big league games, he learned the game of baseball and his famous knuckleball from his father, Phil Sr., a sandlot player in West Virginia. He spent nearly eight years in professional baseball before moving up to the majors on a full-time basis with the Atlanta Braves in 1967, but that was just the beginning of a brilliant career. Phil earned his 300th victory by pitching an 8-0 four-hitter for the New York Yankees against Toronto. At age 46, that made him the oldest major leaguer ever to throw a shutout. Two years and 14 wins later, he called it quits. Prior to accepting the role as the first-ever manager of the Colorado Silver Bullets, Phil had served as a manager and pitching coach for the Richmond Braves AAA franchise.

Joe Niekro

Joe spent 22 years in major league baseball, and while his numbers don't quite add up to those of older brother Phil, he won 221 games for seven different teams during his career. Even more significantly, Joe and Phil combined to win 539 major league games, the most of any brother combination in big league history. Like his older brother, Joe's pitching success was the result of craftiness and guile rather than speed and strength. He baffled batters for more than two decades with an assortment of Niekro knuckle balls and other off-speed offerings. His greatest success came in Houston where he won 155 games in 10 seasons for the Astros. That included back-to-back 20-win seasons in 1979 and 1980. Despite his long and stellar career in the majors, Joe never worked harder or accomplished more than he did as a coach of the Silver Bullets pitching staff in 1994.

John Niekro

John was first exposed to baseball as a toddler while his father, Phil, was pitching for the Atlanta Braves. As might be expected from someone with that type of exposure to the sport, he fell in love with the game at a very early age. Also predictable was the notion that he would indicate a preference toward pitching, and that's what he did best as a youngster. John pitched Shiloh (Georgia) High School to the state AA championship as a senior in 1987. He then pitched four years at Troy State University in Alabama. After receiving his bachelor of science degree in criminal justice in 1992, he spent a year and a half coordinating special events for the Major League Baseball Players Alumni Association, based in Pittsburgh. John was a jack-of-all-trades during the Silver Bullets' inaugural campaign, assisting in numerous areas in addition to his coaching duties.

Tommy Jones

Tommy joined the Silver Bullets after managing for 12 seasons at every level of minor league baseball. A player with eight seasons of professional baseball experience in the San Diego and San Francisco organizations, he launched his managing career in 1982 when he guided Butte to a second place finish in the Pioneer League. He was named Pioneer League Manager-of-the-Year in 1982 and '83, an honor he earned five more times at various minor league stops. Tommy's success gave him a chance to manage All-Star games in Florida State League in 1984 and the Southern League in 1986, but his biggest thrill may have come in 1985 when he was a member of the coaching staff for the World Champion Kansas City Royals. After helping coordinate the Silver Bullets try-out camps and spring training this year, he served as third base coach during the season.

Bob Hope

Colorado Silver Bullets President Bob Hope is a former executive vice-president of Burson-Marsteller, the world's largest public relations firm, and past vice-president of the Atlanta Braves. He has been described by SPORTS ILLUSTRATED as "the most innovative promoter in sports."

Responsible for worldwide marketing at Burson-Marsteller, Hope directed Olympic involvement for major international clients. In addition, he advised cities seeking expansion franchises in professional sports and assisted the successful campaigns of the Charlotte Hornets of the National Basketball Association, the Ottawa Senators of the National Hockey League, and major-league baseball's Florida Marlins.

In 1991, he published WE COULD'VE FINISHED LAST WITHOUT YOU, a personal account of his experiences with the Braves and Hawks. Hope and his wife, Susan, have two daughters, Betsy and Clair.

Paul Beckham

Paul D. Beckham is Chairman of Hope-Beckham, Inc., the media/sports marketing firm based in Atlanta, Georgia, that owns the Silver Bullets.

Prior to acquiring his interest in Hope-Beckham, Beckham was affiliated with Turner Broadcasting System for 23 years.

In 1990, Beckham was drafted by Ted Turner to run the Goodwill Games in Seattle, Washington. This was a $200 million event, staged over a 16-day period and involving 1,500 world-class athletes.

After the Goodwill Games, Beckham assumed the role of President of Turner Cable Network Sales, the sales and marketing arm of Turner Broadcasting responsible for distribution of the Turner product (CNN, WTBS, TNT, etc.) to the cable universe.

Beckham is a lifelong resident of the Atlanta, Georgia, area where he resides with his wife, Cheryl.

Kevin Lewis

Kevin Lewis came to the Silver Bullets after two and a half years with Whittle Events in Knoxville. He graduated from the University of Tennessee in 1989 with a degree in sports management, and loves water-skiing, tennis and roller-blading. Lewis is single and makes his home in Knoxville, Tennessee.

Last year he coordinated travel arrangements and promotional activities for the team.

Kathleen Christie

Kathleen Christie served as director of media relations for the Silver Bullets. A 1991 honors graduate of the University of Tennessee, where she majored in marketing, Kathleen was a member of a basketball team that won a silver medal in the 1984 Junior Olympics. She also competed for many years in volleyball and swimming.

Lynne Boring

Lynne Boring, a native of Orlando, Florida, is trainer for the Silver Bullets. She played competitive volleyball in high school and for two years at the University of South Florida. She graduated in 1993 with a liberal studies degree, specializing in athletic training.

Shereen Samonds

Shereen Samonds was general manager for the Silver Bullets' inaugural season. Before joining the team, she capped six years in professional baseball by being named the 1993 Female Executive of the Year by the National Association of Professional Baseball Leagues. She had been general manager of the AA Orlando (Florida) Cubs since 1990.

Leo Kiely Pete Coors

Leo Kiely throws out first pitch as Peter Coors looks on.

Leo Kiely is president and chief operating officer of Coors Brewing Company — the first non-family member to hold that post. He reports to Peter Coors, vice chairman and chief executive officer. Since joining Coors from Frito-Lay, Inc., in 1993, Kiely has initiated broad managerial and organizational improvements that have improved Coors' business performance. He also has been a strong supporter of the Silver Bullets baseball team. Kiely, an avid reader who enjoys skiing and golf, lives with his family in Golden, Colorado.

Polly Temple

A former personal trainer and a certified aerobics instructor for 11 years, Polly served as administrative assistant for the Silver Bullets.